Mitch to the Rescue

Story by Annette Smith
Illustrations by Mark Wilson

Dad and the boys
got into their canoe.

"Don't drop our new sunhats
in the water," said Ben to Mitch.

"Off we go!" said Dad.

Ben and Dad paddled the canoe.
Mitch held the lunch
and the sunhats.

"Dad, look!" shouted Mitch.
"There's a mother duck
with her ducklings."

"Let's see where they are going,"
said Dad.

"Oh, no!" said Ben.
"The last little duckling
  can't keep up
  with its mother.
The water by the rocks
  is going too fast for it."

"Can we go and help the duckling?"
asked Mitch.
"Please, Dad?"

"Let's stop the canoe
next to the rocks," said Dad,
"and see if we can save
the duckling."

Dad and Ben paddled the canoe
over to the rocks.

"I can see the duckling," said Mitch.
"I'll get it in my sunhat.
I can climb out onto the rocks."

"Be careful, Mitch," said Dad.
"Don't slip."

Mitch climbed onto the rocks and scooped up the duckling in his sunhat.

"Well done, Mitch," said Dad.

Mitch got back into the canoe
with the little duckling.
Dad and Ben began to paddle
across the river.

"I'll keep a lookout
    for the other ducks," said Ben.

Mitch looked at the little duckling.
"We are going to find
your mother for you," he said.

They all looked up and down
the river, but they couldn't see
the ducks anywhere.

"I can see them!" shouted Ben at last. "Look! There they are, under that big tree."

They paddled the canoe to the bank, and the boys climbed out with the duckling.

Ben and Mitch
walked along
the riverbank
to the tree.
"Put your hat
down in the water,
Mitch," said Ben,
"and the duckling
will swim
to its mother."

"There it goes," said Mitch.
"Look, my new hat got wet,
but I saved the duckling."